Working with
paraprofessionals

Julie Sausen

CORWIN

A SAGE Company

CORWIN
A SAGE Company

FOR INFORMATION:

Corwin

A SAGE Company

2455 Teller Road

Thousand Oaks, California 91320

(800) 233-9936

Fax: (800) 417-2466

www.corwin.com

SAGE Ltd.

1 Oliver's Yard

55 City Road

London EC1Y 1SP

United Kingdom

SAGE India Pvt. Ltd.

B 1/I 1 Mohan Cooperative Industrial Area

Mathura Road, New Delhi 110 044

India

SAGE Asia-Pacific Pte. Ltd.

33 Pekin Street #02-01

Far East Square

Singapore 048763

Copyright © 2004 by Corwin

Printed in the United States of America.

ISBN 978-1-5751-7882-0

There are
one-story intellects,
two-story intellects, and
three-story intellects with skylights.

All fact collectors, who have no aim beyond their facts, are

one-story minds.

Two-story minds
compare, reason, generalize,
using the labors of the fact collectors
as well as their own.

Three-story minds
idealize, imagine, predict—their best illumination
comes from above,

through the **skylight.**

—Oliver Wendell Holmes

CORWIN
A SAGE Company

Contents

Understanding the Law

The Individuals with Disabilities Education Act Amendments of 1997 (IDEA '97) specifies "that all children—including those with disabilities formerly excluded from school—were entitled to a free, appropriate public education. This law went far beyond any previous legislation in specifying that, to the greatest extent possible, this 'special' education was to be provided in the least-restrictive environment" (Masterpoli and Scruggs 2000, 3). IDEA '97 and other similar laws increased the number of paraprofessionals and educational assistants in schools and classrooms across the country because the "least restrictive environment" is usually the general education classroom.

The adoption of IDEA '97 started what Masterpoli and Scruggs (2000) call the "full inclusion" movement (21). School administrations across the country must abide by the inclusion laws and place students with special needs in classrooms that are considered to be the least restrictive learning environment. In many cases, the general education classroom is considered the least restrictive environment to learn content and to provide social interactions for students with special needs. When the least restrictive environment for a student is defined as the general education classroom, the student is placed in that classroom for the entire school day. The full inclusion movement allows for many students with different types of disabilities to be placed in the same general education classroom.

Placing students in the least restrictive environment creates challenges for the administration of school districts with limited classes, many novice teachers, and few resource services, such as reading and math specialists. In some districts, it is not always possible to place students with special needs with experienced teachers and paraprofessionals—someone who helps a certified educator in the general education classroom—because of scheduling conflicts or insufficient resources. Moreover, in school districts with high attrition rates, students with disabilities may be placed in classrooms of first- or second-year teachers who may have little or no training in special or gifted education. Working with special needs students and a paraprofessional in the classroom adds new challenges to a first- or second-year teacher's assignment. The new teacher is already unfamiliar with the school and curriculum. Adding paraprofessionals requires them to familiarize themselves with laws and strategies for working effectively with other adults in the classroom.

"**S**tudents with disabilities bring a spectrum of expectations to the school experience. Each student possesses unique learning characteristics that will possibly challenge the instructor and can potentially cause the school experience to be one of devastation for the student" (Shelton and Pollingue 2000, 23). To meet the challenges of students with special needs and to avoid difficulty for the students, a paraprofessional can assist the teacher in guiding one or many students in the development of academic and social skills. The paraprofessional may work in any one of the following situations:

- **General**—The paraprofessional can be a generalist, who assists all students in a classroom.
- **Small Group of Students to One**—The paraprofessional may be specialized in a specific area such as reading, math, a specific learning disability, or gifted and talented. This paraprofessional is assigned to a small group of students with similar learning needs.
- **One-to-One**—The paraprofessional may be assigned to a specific student with special needs, usually with an individual education plan (IEP) in a general education classroom.

Figures 1 and 2 are examples of classroom situations teachers and paraprofessionals may encounter. (See also Blackline 1 at the end of this book. Teachers can use this blackline master to determine their classroom situation and their paraprofessional needs.)

Elementary/Middle School Situation

My current classroom situation is…
   This year in my fifth grade classroom I have 30 students. I have 5 specific learning disability (SLD) students who have individual education plans (IEPs). Each student has a different set of goals and expectations. All 5 students are reading below grade level; math is a problem for 2 of the 5 students. I have a paraprofessional to assist me in the classroom, as well as having help from reading and math specialists.

My paraprofessional situation is…
   My paraprofessional assists me by working with a small group of students. She helps them to organize tasks and assignments, track their schedules when leaving the room for reading or math, and assist them in troublesome situations. The paraprofessional assists SLD students one-to-one when conducting an assessment, building vocabulary skills, or working on individual math problems.
   My paraprofessional is gone 40 minutes a day between 11:00 and 11:40 to assist with lunch and recess duty.

Figure 1

Middle/High School Situation

My current classroom situation is…

> This year, I have three 55-minute tenth-grade western history classes and two 55-minute ninth-grade American history classes. In my third period tenth-grade class, I have one student with a traumatic brain injury who has an individualized educational plan (IEP). This student is guided to classes with the assistance of a one-to-one paraprofessional. She has a motorized wheelchair, so space must be provided for her when setting up the classroom.

My paraprofessional situation is…

> The paraprofessional assists me in situations that include working with this student one-to-one. The paraprofessional assists this student when participating in cooperative group activities, field trips, history simulations, and other projects. The paraprofessional also guides the student through activities that are designed to help her achieve her IEP goals and create a learning environment that is enriching for her.

Figure 2

Paraprofessional Roles and Responsibilities

As Morgan and Ashbaker (2001) point out, "Some classroom responsibilities belong to the teacher alone, whereas others can be shared. Within the legal limits imposed by your state and district, you need to consider which responsibilities must remain yours as a teacher and which ones you may share with your paraeducator or other adult who works with you" (19). Whether dictated by law or classroom needs, there are specific tasks that a paraprofessional can and cannot perform in the classroom. "When a paraprofessional is assigned to a teacher or classroom to assist students with special needs it is crucial that they are viewed as a support for all students" (McVay 1998, 3). The major role of a paraprofessional in the classroom is to provide extra educational support to the teacher and students.

Guiding students who have Individualized Education Plans (IEPs) and supporting teachers are the roles of the paraprofessional, but he or she is not the sole responsible party in making sure students achieve their goals. It is the certified educator's responsibility to keep track of individual student achievements and create a learning environment that allows all students to achieve their highest potential. To avoid problems with specific tasks a paraprofessional can and cannot perform, it is good practice for teachers to review and keep current on specific laws that refer to particular situations involving paraprofessionals. If a new teacher is unsure if a task is appropriate for a paraprofessional, the teacher can ask a mentor or administrator. The paraprofessional should not be assigned tasks that put a student in danger.

Careful planning will help beginning teachers avoid problems when assigning tasks to paraprofessionals. Figure 3 is a sample paraprofessional task planner that demonstrates the benefits of planning. (A blackline master of the planner appears at the end of this book.) After completing the paraprofessional task planner, a teacher can review the plan for potential problems. For example, if the plan has a paraprofessional alone without a certified staff member, the teacher can reassign the task to a certified task member or redesign the task so the paraprofessional will not be alone.

When developing the paraprofessional-to-teacher relationship and setting tasks and responsibilities, it is important for teachers to be familiar with current laws and know the needs of individual students. Clear assignments of paraprofessional responsibilities establish trust early in the relationship and avoid miscommunications.

Establishing Collaboration

A large part of establishing a strong working relationship depends on communication and collaboration between the teacher and the paraprofessional. "Collaboration is the process of developing interdependent relationships where all are focused on a common purpose and set of goals and where people must rely on one another to achieve these goals. It is the synergy created when a group's effectiveness exceeds what individuals can accomplish on their own" (Conzemius and O'Neill 2001, 15–16). The difficult part of collaboration, however, is finding time to plan together. Educators' duties reach beyond the classroom walls before and after school. During the school day, teachers find little time to eat lunch, much less collaborate with their paraprofessionals who might have a different schedule. Educators may be able to find time for collaboration without sacrificing other duties. For example, when teachers at Monona Grove High School were challenged to find collaboration time without increasing the budget or

Sample Paraprofessional Task Planner

1. **Task:** Read a short story to 4 students with reading difficulties.

2. **Purpose of the task:** Read a chapter and ask questions at the end of the reading to check for comprehension skills.

3. **The task involves:** records (paper)   one student   (multiple students)

4. **Steps for Completing the Task** / **Person Completing the Task**

Steps for Completing the Task	Person Completing the Task
a. Select the next chapter in the book.	Teacher
b. Create questions that encourage higher-order thinking.	Teacher
c. Explain the task to the paraprofessional.	Teacher
d. Four students will go to the school library to read.	Paraprofessional
e. Discuss reading with students and encourage conversation.	Paraprofessional
f. Students complete the comprehension questions with guidance.	Paraprofessional
g. Students' work reported back to the teacher.	Paraprofessional
h. Work is graded and recorded in the gradebook.	Teacher

5. Does the task meet or complete a student's IEP goal?   (Yes)   No

6. Do any of the steps require the paraprofessional to be alone without a certified staff member in the classroom with a student or group of students?
   The library has two certified adults, so this will not be an issue.

7. Is the safety of any students put at risk anytime during the steps of the task?   No

8. Is there a step for the certified educator to monitor the task?   Yes, in the library

9. What is the role of the paraprofessional?   (assistant)   facilitator   teacher?

10. What steps will the paraprofessional take to report the activities of the task back to the teacher?
    a. Paraprofessional will discuss with teacher the processes that took place from notes that are taken.
    b. Paraprofessional will give completed student work to teacher for recording.

Figure 3

taking time away from student learning, educators came up with a list within five minutes (see Figure 4).

Many teachers do not have the authority to make decisions about the length of the school day or when their classes attend physical education, art, music, or foreign language classes. However, teachers can brainstorm a list of ways to collaborate with others within the district's parameters. Defining the collaboration plan opens the discussion for ideas that could be incorporated into the district's strategic plan. Administrators could consider involving a group of teachers from different areas within the school building during the brainstorming session. Involving a wide range of staff members in the brainstorming session results in more ownership by the staff and promotes school-wide collaboration. School staff meetings are suitable for discussing and planning brainstorming sessions.

Find Collaboration Time

- Combine individual planning time into collaborative time.
- Rearrange teachers' preparation time or class schedules so that each teacher's class attends physical education, art, or music class at the same time allowing, the teachers of the same grade to plan together while the students are away.
- Have previous grade teachers take back their classes every two weeks. In other words, fourth grade students may partner up with fifth grade students for a group science activity, reading buddies, or research project. During this time, the fourth grade teachers have an opportunity to plan together.
- Move the academic start time back one hour and plan meaningful student activities during that time. Activities may include environmental awareness, technology, reading, orchestra/band, choir, debate, math, or tutoring other students.
- Create sectionals or groups of classes with similar schedules and have certified support staff take charge of students and discuss issues such as safety and community service.
- Hold monthly career exploration days where community members present to the students in large assembly.
- Create an enrichment team of certified support teachers (physical education, music, art, school psychologist, reading teacher, math teacher, etc.) to work with classrooms of students on a rotating basis.

(Adapted from Conzemius and O'Neill 2001, 70. Used with permission.)

Figure 4

Preparing Before School Begins

Ensuring that having a paraprofessional in the classroom will work requires the teacher to consider a number of issues before school begins. The teacher and paraprofessional should discuss workspace issues, classroom rules and procedures, schedules, and roles and responsibilities of the adults and the students. By discussing these issues before school begins, the teacher avoids problems and miscommunications once classes start. It is important that the classroom teacher and the paraprofessional present a "united front" on the first day of classes.

The Welcome Meeting

A successful relationship between the teacher and paraprofessional begins with an initial meeting. In this meeting, it is important to define the roles and responsibilities of both the teacher and the paraprofessional before the students enter the classroom. Even though the teacher assumes the role as primary person responsible for the classroom, the paraprofessional must feel a sense of partnership and assume some ownership of the responsibilities of the classroom community. The initial meeting can be an invitation to stop by or a formal meeting with an agenda of items to discuss. Since the paraprofessional may be nervous about his or her role, a meeting invitation from the teacher can serve as a preliminary step in establishing an ongoing collaborative relationship. The Welcome Meeting Checklist (Figure 5) provides guidance during an initial meeting with a paraprofessional. The checklist can be adapted to accommodate additional roles and responsibilities the district may require.

Workspace

A workspace should be set up for the paraprofessional so that he or she can work with one student or a group of students in the classroom. The paraprofessional needs a space to assist students or to fill out paperwork, but the workspace should not isolate the paraprofessional from the teacher. After the physical classroom space is set up, the teacher should invite the paraprofessional to the classroom to see it.

Welcome Meeting Checklist

_____ Introductions

_____ Tour of Classroom

_____ Tour of School

_____ Review the Situations Sheet

Roles

Teacher	Paraprofessional	Students

Responsibilities

Teacher	Paraprofessional	Students

Next Meeting Time _____

Teacher: _____   Paraprofessional: _____

Figure 5

Exploring a Five-Step Process for Special Education

"The teaching of students with disabilities is a monumental task that requires a tremendous amount of preparation" (Shelton and Pollingue 2000, 81). Well-prepared teachers face a challenging situation more confidently if they have an action plan. Shelton and Pollingue (2000) have created a five-step process (see Figure 6) that simplifies preparation for teachers of special education.

Step One: Review Students' Needs and Goals

Teachers need to be familiar with the needs and goals of individual students. Before school begins, teachers should review students' IEPs or other educational plans in the students' files. For example, a 504 plan is created for students who do not meet the requirements to be served under IDEA but qualify for special needs services through Section 504, which provides equal opportunities for all students in education. A 504 plan would be created for students who have attention deficit disorder (ADD), attention deficit hyperactivity disorder (ADHD), severe allergies, or other medical conditions not served under IDEA (Masterpoli and Scruggs 2000, 13).

Five-Step Process for Special Education

Step One
Review each student's IEP and identify academic goals and objectives that need to be addressed throughout the year.

Step Two
Review and select appropriate instructional materials that support the curriculum and challenge the needs of the students with disabilities.

Step Three
Create a class schedule that is accommodating to all students.

Step Four
Create a classroom environment that is suitable for all students to learn.

Step Five
Develop lesson plans that help students to process, practice, and learn information in exciting ways.

Adapted from C. F. Shelton and A. B. Pollingue. 2000. *The exceptional teacher's handbook: The first-year special education teacher's guide for success.* Thousand Oaks, CA: Corwin Press. A Sage Publications Company. Reprinted with permission.

Figure 6

Student plans are designed to meet the needs of the special education laws. "Students who have been referred to special education must have an individualized education plan (IEP) that details their special learning needs and mandates appropriate services. Short- and long-term goals and objectives are listed explicitly on IEPs" (Masterpoli and Scruggs 2000, 16). Before setting up a second meeting with the paraprofessional, the teacher should review these plans. When reviewing the plans, the teacher can note specific information for each student in a chart to keep goals and needs organized (see Figure 7 for a sample chart). Once the students' needs have been organized, the teacher can share them with the paraprofessional so both parties have the same information and share the same goals to help each student.

Step Two: Find Resources and Materials

After reviewing the IEPs, the next step is to find resources and materials that help students reach their goals. This task requires the assistance of a paraprofessional, because the classroom teacher has 20–30 other students who also need resources and materials. Using the Overview of Student Needs and Goals (a sample is shown in Figure 8 and a blackline master is provided at the end of this book), teachers and paraprofessionals survey the classroom and create a list of books, supplemental materials, and supplies that will help students accomplish their goals. Figure 7 lists items that are normally found in classrooms. (Blackline 4 at the end of this book can

Classroom Resources and Materials

Elementary/Middle School
- Tape player/recorder with headphones
- Calculators
- Counting blocks
- Picture books
- Vocabulary cards
- Educational software
- Alphabet chart
- Number line
- Assignment board
- Dictionaries

Middle/High School
- Tape recorder with headphones
- Calculators/graphing calculators
- Dictionaries
- Educational software
- Writing charts (paragraphs, editorial)
- Assignment board

Figure 7

Sample Overview of Student Needs and Goals

Student Name	Need Identified by Educational Plan	Learning Strategies Identified by Educational Plan	Goals Identified by Educational Plan
John	Attention Deficit Disorder	• Extra time on written tests in reading • Written directions • Behavior Modification Contract	• Increase vocabulary word set by 75+ new words • Understand written directions • Be able to walk to classes without problems and arrive on time
Amy	Hearing loss	• Desk close to teacher • Small group work for redirections	• Work on sounds *ch, sh, th, k,* and hard/soft *c* • Read small passage aloud • Increase social skills in small group work
Katie	Gifted and Talented	• Enrichment problems in math • Gifted group meeting once a week	• Complete next grade-level math problems • Work well in cooperative groups (giving others a chance to complete work)
Suzanne	ESL	• Read written tests aloud • Small group work • Reading group for 60 minutes, 4 times a week	• Increase vocabulary • Increase comprehension skills through a variety of strategies

Figure 8

be used to record resources and materials that will help students accomplish their goals.) To use the list as an aid when planning, teachers can post the list in a place where paraprofessionals have easy access to it.

Step Three: Create Schedules

Once the teacher and paraprofessional determine their roles and responsibilities and students' needs, they should decide on a daily routine. Creating and posting a classroom schedule helps teachers and paraprofessionals stay focused on meeting the needs of their students. "The class schedule provides class structure, ensures that instruction time for the core academic areas is maximized, and integrates lower priority classes with other miscellaneous activities" (Shelton and Pollingue 2000, 86). Scheduling, however, can be very difficult. The paraprofessional may work with many students and some students may see other specialists throughout the school day. The district or school administrator may also have additional duties for the paraprofessional to do during the school day. Paraprofessionals are often assigned bus or lunchroom duty or asked to proctor a study hall. Creating a schedule as a collaborative team can help teachers and paraprofessionals set priorities and plan how the classroom will operate. It is best if the teacher and paraprofessional complete individual schedules first and then meet to create a combined one. Times for planning and communicating must also be included. Teachers and paraprofessionals should regularly meet to review the schedule and keep it updated. There will always be changes and emergencies, but it is important to begin the year with a mutually agreed upon schedule. (For schedules that are organized and easy to read, see Blacklines 5 and 6 at the end of this book.)

Step Four: Create a Positive Learning Environment

When establishing a positive learning environment in the classroom, teachers begin by reflecting on their students' goals. "Students appear to pursue learning content most energetically if they are involved along with the teacher in establishing cognitive group agreements that deal with the processes of learning" (Schmuck and Schmuck 1997, 201). Students learn when they are excited about content that relates to their lives.

If students are involved in the learning process they will be more interested in the content. Although students may not always be included in planning, it is important to include students in the teaching and learning process. As cited in Renck-Jalongo (1991), "Goodlad's (1984) study *A Place Called School* found that opportunities for interaction are regarded by adolescents as the major reason for being in school. Rather than fighting this need for affiliation, educators need to harness its energy to promote learning" (41). Teachers and paraprofessionals can implement the following strategies to harness student energy and engage students:

- Cooperative groups
- Graphic organizers
- Gardner's multiple intelligences
- Thematic instruction
- Experiential learning activities
- Guest speakers
- Cross-age tutoring (students teaching other students from different grade levels)

See Blackline 7 for a blackline master that teachers can use to plan positive learning environments for their students.

Step Five: Develop Lesson Plans and Monitor Student Progress

It is important for beginning teachers to know that the teacher, not the paraprofessional, has primary responsibility for the achievement and goals of the students. Although they can assist a teacher in planning and carrying out activities that help students achieve goals, paraprofessionals are not responsible for the students' achievement. Often, paraprofessionals are uncertified parents or community members who want to be involved in the school.

By law, achievement goals must align with a student's IEP. If a student is not on a specific plan and needs help, then careful review of the student's file, past work, and input from others can be considered when setting goals. Planning achievement goals is very personal to each student. Teachers and paraprofessionals need to be sensitive to the student's feelings and keep the student's privacy in mind. "It is always helpful to know where your students need enrichment. However, you must remember not to share specific information that would be violating a confidence" (Rosenblum-Lowden 2000, 137).

When planning lessons geared to students' achievement goals, the teacher and paraprofessional can document students' progress with individual student goal sheets. Individual student goal sheets work well with students with IEPs or 504 plans. Goal sheets can be kept on a weekly basis. Recording student progress tracks what the student has accomplished during the week and what needs to be accomplished during the upcoming weeks.

The paraprofessional can be assigned the task of recording student progress. The detailed records of individual student goal sheets facilitate communication of students' progress between a teacher and paraprofessional. At the end of the week, the teacher should review each student goal sheet and discuss the recorded information with the paraprofessional. Using the recorded information, the teacher and paraprofessional can create new sheets and plan students' goals for the next week. By reviewing individual student goal sheets, teachers assess the paraprofessional's accomplishments with students, stay current on students' progress, and make informed choices when planning lessons that meet students' needs and goals. By discussing the recorded information on individual student goal sheets with the paraprofessional, the teacher avoids misunderstanding and miscommunications with paraprofessionals and with students. These goal sheets can also be used at parent/teacher conferences to show a record of students' progress. See Figure 9 for a sample individual student goal sheet; see Blackline 8 at the end of this selection for a blackline master.

Teachers and paraprofessionals of special education students benefit from thorough planning. The five-step process Shelton and Pollingue (2000) created gives educators a framework for planning. "The completion of these steps should maximize student performance and teacher effectiveness" (Shelton and Pollingue 2000, 81).

Sample Individual Student Goal Sheet

Student Name: _____ Susan _____   Week of: _____ 3/22 _____

Date/Topic	Goal	Activity	Accomplished	Needs to Be Worked On
3/18 Math	Master multiplication facts—tens, elevens, and twelves Part of goal 2 on IEP	Multiplication software on the computer	Susan accomplished levels nine and ten on the software program. Level nine covered multiplying numbers by nines, tens, and elevens. Level ten covered multiplying by tens, elevens, and twelves.	Susan has mastered the tens. She needs to continue working on her multiplication facts for elevens and twelves.
3/19 Literacy	Understand the meaning of unknown words from the reading chapter Part of goal 1 on IEP	Read chapter 2 and create a list of words that are unknown from the reading chapter	Susan read through chapter 2 and we discussed what was in the chapter. She created her list of words.	Susan needs to understand the meaning of the words and how they are used in a sentence.
3/20 Math	Master division facts—tens, elevens, and twelves Part of goal 2 on IEP	Small group division flash card activity Part of goal 3 on IEP	Susan completed the tens and elevens and did really well. She has tens mastered.	Susan needs to continue working on elevens and twelves.
3/21 Social Studies	Work together with 2 other students on a small group project Part of goal 3 on IEP	Work on a research project with two other students in the class	Susan and her group created a task sheet for what the group would like to accomplish next in the research.	The group decided that next on the task list would be organizing their research into categories. Susan will participate in this task.
3/22 Literacy	Understand the meaning of unknown words from reading chapter book Part of goal 1 on IEP	Find the meanings of the unknown words in the electronic dictionary	Susan looked up 7 of her 7 words in the electronic dictionary.	Susan needs to put each of these words in new sentences that have meaning to her.

Figure 9

Even in a well-planned, trusting teacher/paraprofessional relationship, conflicts will arise. The teacher and the paraprofessional bring different skills and experiences into the relationship, and it is important to remember that the contribution of each person is of value. "Your paraeducator, as an adult learner, has a wealth of experience and knowledge, even though that experience may not be in education or related to children" (Morgan and Ashbaker 2001, 51). The teacher and the paraprofessional may have different pedagogical views. The paraprofessional also may have a different discipline style from the teacher. Moreover, a miscommunication in student progress could spark a conflict.

Regardless of the conflict source, the conflict must be handled professionally and quickly. The focus of the teacher/paraprofessional relationship is, after all, the student. Since the teacher is primarily responsible for the students' progress, the teacher must be straightforward and clear with the paraprofessional when resolving a conflict. As discussed earlier, the teacher must establish a positive working relationship with the paraprofessional. Although a trusting relationship may be developed, communication is a process and must be nurtured. Because miscommunication is often the cause of a conflict, it is important for the teacher to state what is expected from the paraprofessional at the beginning. Compromise will be more attainable if everyone has a clear understanding of expectations.

To resolve conflicts, educators need to be objective and work for a compromise. Meridith (2000) recommends a "win-win" approach. Adhering to an approach where one person "loses" will result in negative feelings and make future collaborations difficult. Maintaining a win-win approach will enable teachers and paraprofessionals to continue a positive relationship. See Figure 10 for steps to resolve conflict.

Steps for Resolving Conflict

1. **Assess the situation.**

   Is the situation something that can be addressed in a one-on-one conversation?

   Is there a bigger issue involved where a mediator may be of assistance?

2. **Talk to the paraprofessional.**

   The teacher and the paraprofessional are both individuals with their own ideas and methods. Misunderstandings can often be resolved by talking things out.

3. **Use a mediator.**

   If the situation cannot be resolved by talking, bring in another paraprofessional, teacher, or an outsider who can help resolve the issue. Another staff member may have a new, objective idea for resolving the issue.

4. **Talk to an administrator.**

   If a teacher has tried to resolve the issue in every way possible, or if the issue involves violating the law, the teacher should talk to the administrator who can address the problem immediately.

Figure 10

Conclusion

The teacher is responsible for the safety and learning of the students within the classroom. "You are the leader of your classroom instructional team, and you can be as creative as you wish in deciding how best to use your paraeducator's skills and strengths. There are no standard roles for paraeducators and no standard procedures for effective supervision" (Morgan and Ashbaker 2000, 87). A paraprofessional and a teacher can make a dynamic team that maximizes student achievement; however, the teacher is always the person leading the team.

Reproducible Blacklines

Classroom Situation

My current classroom situation is . . .

My paraprofessional will…

Teacher:_____   Date: _____

Paraprofessional Task Planner

1. Task: _____

2. Purpose of the task: _____

   _____

   _____

3. The task involves: **records (paper)**   **one student**   **multiple students**

4.   **Steps for Completing the Task**   **Person Completing the Task**

   a. _____ | _____

   b. _____ | _____

   c. _____ | _____

   d. _____ | _____

   e. _____ | _____

   f. _____ | _____

   g. _____ | _____

   h. _____ | _____

5. Does the task meet or complete a student's IEP goal?   **Yes**   **No**

6. Do any of the steps require the paraprofessional to be alone without a certified staff member in the classroom with a student or group of students?

7. Is the safety of any student put at risk anytime during the steps of the task?

8. Is there a step for the certified educator to monitor the task?

9. The role of the paraprofessional: **assistant**   **facilitator**   **teacher**

10. What steps will the paraprofessional take to report the activities of the task back to the teacher?

   a. _____

   b. _____

   c. _____

Blackline 2

Overview of Student Needs and Goals

Teacher:_____ Class:_____ Date:_____

Student Name	Needs Identified by Educational Plan	Goals Identified by Educational Plan

Blackline 3

List of Resources and Materials

Teacher:_____ Class/Grade:_____ Date:_____

Student Name	Student Goals	Available Books	Available Manipulatives

Blackline 4

Paraprofessional Schedule

Teacher: _____

Paraprofessional: _____　　Class/Grade: _____　　Date: _____

Time	Monday	Tuesday	Wednesday	Thursday	Friday

Student Daily Schedule

Name of Student: _____ Class/Grade: _____ Date: _____

Time	Monday	Tuesday	Wednesday	Thursday	Friday

Blackline 6

Strategies to Achieve Student Goals

Teacher:_____ Paraprofessional:_____ Course/Class:_____ Date:_____

Student Name	Student Need	Instructional Strategy or Tool

Sample Individual Student Goal Sheet

Student Name: _____

Week of: _____

Date/Topic	Goal	Activity	Accomplished	Needs to Be Worked On

BIBLIOGRAPHY

Association of Supervision and Curriculum Development. 1995. The inclusive school (Special Issue). *Educational Leadership,* 52(4).

Baker, J., and N. Zigmond. 1990. Are regular education classes equipped to accommodate students with learning disabilities? Exceptional Children 56, 515–526.

Banks, J.A., and C. A. Banks. Eds. 1997. *Multicultural education: Issues and perspectives.* Boston: Allyn and Bacon.

Carroll, D. 2001. Considering paraeducator training, roles, and responsibilities. In *Exceptional Children* 34(2):60–64.

Conzemius, A. and J. O'Neill. 2001. *Building shared responsibility for student learning.* Alexandria, VA: Association for Supervision and Curriculum Development.

Doyle, M. B. 1998. My child has a new shadow…and it doesn't resemble her! *Disability Solutions* 3(1):5–9.

Falvey, M. 1995. *Inclusive and heterogeneous schooling: Assessment, curriculum, and instruction.* Baltimore, MD: Paul H. Brookes.

French, N. 1999. Supervising paraeducators—What every teacher should know. *CEC Today Online* 6(2):1–2.

Friend, M., and W. D. Bursuck. Eds. (1999). *Including students with special needs: A practical guide for classroom teacher,* 2nd ed. Boston: Allyn & Bacon.

Giangreco, M. F., S. W. Edelman, S. M. Broer, and M. B. Doyle. 2001. Paraprofessional support of students with disablilities: Literature from the past decade. In *Council for Exceptional Children* 68(1):45–63.

Goodlad, J. I. 1984. *A place called school: Promise for the future.* New York: McGraw-Hill Professional Publishing.

Gordon, S. P. and S. Maxey. 2000. *How to help beginning teachers succeed,* 2nd ed. Alexandria, VA: Association for Curriculum and Supervision.

Jones, V. F. and L. S. Jones. 1998. *Comprehensive classroom management: Creating communities of support and solving problems.* Needham MA: Allyn and Bacon.

Jorgensen, C. M. 1998. *Restructuring high schools for all students: Taking inclusion to the next level.* Baltimore, MD: Paul H. Brookes Publishing.

La Brecque, R. J. 1998. *Effective department and team leaders: A practical guide.* Norwood, MA: Christopher-Gordon Publishers.

Lipsky, D. K., and A. Gartner. 1997. *Inclusion and school reform: Transforming America's classrooms.* Baltimore, MD: Paul H. Brookes Publishing.

Masterpoli, M. A. and T. E. Scruggs. 2000. *The inclusive classroom: Strategies for effective instruction.* Upper Saddle River, NJ: Merrill.

McVay, P. 1998. Paraprofessionals in the classroom: What role do they play? In *Disability Solutions* 3(1):1–4.

Merideth, E. M. 2000. Leadership strategies for teachers. Arlington Heights, IL: SkyLight Training and Publishing.

Morgan, J. and B. Y. Ashbaker. 2001. *A teacher's guide to working with paraeducators and other classroom aides.* Alexandria VA: Association for Supervision and Curriculum Development.

Power-deFur, L. S., and F. P. Orelove. 1997. *Inclusive education: Practical implementation of the least restrictive environment.* Gaithersburg, MD: Aspen Publishers.

Renck-Jalongo, M. 1991. *Creating learning communities: The role of the teacher in the 21st century.* Bloomington, IN: National Educational Service.

Riveria-Pedrotty, D., and D. Smith-Deutsch. 1997. *Teaching students with learning and behavior problems,* 3rd ed. Needham MA: Allyn and Bacon.

Rosenblum-Lowden, R. 2000. *You have to go to school—You're the teacher!* 2nd Ed. Thousand Oaks, CA: Corwin Press.

Schmuck, R. A., and P. A. Schmuck. 1997. *Group processes in the classroom.* Madison, WI: Brown & Benchmark.

Shelton, C. F. and A. B. Pollingue. 2000. *The exceptional teacher's handbook: The first-year special education teacher's guide for success.* Thousand Oaks, CA: Corwin Press.

Spear-Swerling, L., and R. J. Sternberg. 1998. Curing our 'epidemic' of learning disablilities. *Phi Delta Kappan* 81(5): 397–401.

Tateyama-Sniezek, K. 1990. Cooperative learning: Does it improve the academic achievement of student with handicaps? *Exceptional Children* 56(5): 426–437.

Vaughn, S., C. S. Bos, and J. S. Schumm. 2000. *Teaching exceptional, diverse and at-risk students in the general education classroom,* 2nd ed. Boston: Allyn & Bacon.

Zionts, P. Ed. 1997. *Inclusion strategies for students with learning and behavior problems: Perspectives, experiences, and best practices.* Austin, TX: Pro-Ed.

Notes

Notes

Notes

Notes

Notes

Notes

CORWIN

A SAGE Company

The Corwin logo—a raven striding across an open book—represents the union of courage and learning. Corwin is committed to improving education for all learners by publishing books and other professional development resources for those serving the field of PreK–12 education. By providing practical, hands-on materials, Corwin continues to carry out the promise of its motto: **"Helping Educators Do Their Work Better."**

Printed in the United States
By Bookmasters